DANTE

THE FIRST T[...]LES

TRA[...]

[...]TERS

PENGUIN BOOKS

PENGUIN BOOKS

Published by the Penguin Group
Penguin Books Ltd, 27 Wrights Lane, London w8 5tz, England
Penguin Books USA Inc., 375 Hudson Street, New York, New York 10014, USA
Penguin Books Australia Ltd, Ringwood, Victoria, Australia
Penguin Books Canada Ltd, 10 Alcorn Avenue, Toronto, Ontario, Canada m4v 3b2
Penguin Books (NZ) Ltd, 182–190 Wairau Road, Auckland 10, New Zealand

Penguin Books Ltd, Registered Offices: Harmondsworth, Middlesex, England

These extracts are from Dorothy L. Sayers's translation of Dante's *Inferno*, first
published in Penguin Classics 1949
This edition published 1996
1 3 5 7 9 10 8 6 4 2

Filmset by Datix International Ltd, Bungay, Suffolk
Printed in England by Clays Ltd, St Ives plc

CONTENTS

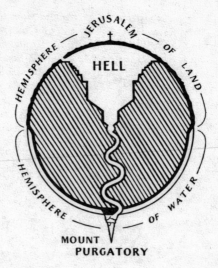

Canto I

THE STORY. *Dante finds that he has strayed from the right road and is lost in a Dark Wood. He tries to escape by climbing a beautiful Mountain, but is turned aside, first by a gambolling Leopard, then by a fierce Lion, and finally by a ravenous She-Wolf. As he is fleeing back into the wood, he is stopped by the shade of Virgil, who tells him that he cannot hope to pass the Wolf and ascend the Mountain by that road. One day a Greyhound will come and drive the Wolf back to Hell; but the only course at present left open to Dante is to trust himself to Virgil, who will guide him by a longer way, leading through Hell and Purgatory. From there, a worthier spirit than Virgil (Beatrice) will lead him on to see the blessed souls in Paradise. Dante accepts Virgil as his 'master, leader, and lord', and they set out together.*

Midway this way of life we're bound upon,
   I woke to find myself in a dark wood,
   Where the right road was wholly lost and gone.

Ay me! how hard to speak of it – that rude   4
   And rough and stubborn forest! the mere breath
   Of memory stirs the old fear in the blood;

It is so bitter, it goes nigh to death;   7
   Yet there I gained such good, that, to convey
   The tale, I'll write what else I found therewith.

10 How I got into it I cannot say,
        Because I was so heavy and full of sleep
        When first I stumbled from the narrow way;

13 But when at last I stood beneath a steep
        Hill's side, which closed that valley's wandering maze
        Whose dread had pierced me to the heart-root deep,

16 Then I looked up, and saw the morning rays
        Mantle its shoulder from that planet bright
        Which guides men's feet aright on all their ways;

19 And this a little quieted the affright
        That lurking in my bosom's lake had lain
        Through the long horror of that piteous night.

22 And as a swimmer, panting, from the main
        Heaves safe to shore, then turns to face the drive
        Of perilous seas, and looks, and looks again,

25 So, while my soul yet fled, did I contrive
        To turn and gaze on that dread pass once more
        Whence no man yet came ever out alive.

28 Weary of limb I rested a brief hour,
        Then rose and onward through the desert hied,
        So that the fixed foot always was the lower;

31 And see! not far from where the mountain-side
        First rose, a Leopard, nimble and light and fleet,
        Clothed in a fine furred pelt all dapple-dyed,

34 Came gambolling out, and skipped before my feet,
        Hindering me so, that from the forthright line
        Time and again I turned to beat retreat.

The morn was young, and in his native sign   37
   The Sun climbed with the stars whose glitterings
   Attended on him when the Love Divine

First moved those happy, prime-created things: 40
   So the sweet season and the new-born day
   Filled me with hope and cheerful augurings

Of the bright beast so speckled and so gay;   43
   Yet not so much but that I fell to quaking
   At a fresh sight – a Lion in the way.

I saw him coming, swift and savage, making   46
   For me, head high, with ravenous hunger raving
   So that for dread the very air seemed shaking.

And next, a Wolf, gaunt with the famished craving   49
   Lodged ever in her horrible lean flank,
   The ancient cause of many men's enslaving; –

She was the worst – at that dread sight a blank   52
   Despair and whelming terror pinned me fast,
   Until all hope to scale the mountain sank.

Like one who loves the gains he has amassed,   55
   And meets the hour when he must lose his loot,
   Distracted in his mind and all aghast,

Even so was I, faced with that restless brute   58
   Which little by little edged and thrust me back,
   Back, to that place wherein the sun is mute.

Then, as I stumbled headlong down the track,   61
   Sudden a form was there, which dumbly crossed
   My path, as though grown voiceless from long lack

64   Of speech; and seeing it in that desert lost,
      'Have pity on me!' I hailed it as I ran,
      'Whate'er thou art – or very man, or ghost!'

67   It spoke: 'No man, although I once was man;
      My parents' native land was Lombardy
      And both by citizenship were Mantuan.

70   *Sub Julio* born, though late in time, was I,
      And lived at Rome in good Augustus' days,
      When the false gods were worshipped ignorantly.

73   Poet was I, and tuned my verse to praise
      Anchises' righteous son, who sailed from Troy
      When Ilium's pride fell ruined down ablaze.

76   But thou – oh, why run back where fears destroy
      Peace? Why not climb the blissful mountain yonder,
      The cause and first beginning of all joy?'

79   'Canst thou be Virgil? thou that fount of splendour
      Whence poured so wide a stream of lordly speech?'
      Said I, and bowed my awe-struck head in wonder;

82   'O honour and light of poets all and each,
      Now let my great love stead me – the bent brow
      And long hours pondering all thy book can teach!

85   Thou art my master, and my author thou,
      From thee alone I learned the singing strain,
      The noble style, that does me honour now.

88   See there the beast that turned me back again –
      Save me from her, great sage – I fear her so,
      She shakes my blood through every pulse and vein.'

'Nay, by another path thou needs must go
   If thou wilt ever leave this waste,' he said,
   Looking upon me as I wept, 'for lo!   91

The savage brute that makes thee cry for dread   94
   Lets no man pass this road of hers, but still
   Trammels him, till at last she lays him dead.

Vicious her nature is, and framed for ill;   97
   When crammed she craves more fiercely than before;
   Her raging greed can never gorge its fill.

With many a beast she mates, and shall with more,   100
   Until the Greyhound come, the Master-hound,
   And he shall slay her with a stroke right sore.

He'll not eat gold nor yet devour the ground;   103
   Wisdom and love and power his food shall be,
   His birthplace between Feltro and Feltro found;

Saviour he'll be to that low Italy   106
   For which Euryalus and Nisus died,
   Turnus and chaste Camilla, bloodily.

He'll hunt the Wolf through cities far and wide,   109
   Till in the end he hunt her back to Hell,
   Whence Envy first of all her leash untied.

But, as for thee, I think and deem it well   112
   Thou take me for thy guide, and pass with me
   Through an eternal place and terrible

Where thou shalt hear despairing cries, and see   115
   Long-parted souls that in their torments dire
   Howl for the second death perpetually.

118   Next, thou shalt gaze on those who in the fire
            Are happy, for they look to mount on high,
            In God's good time, up to the blissful quire;

121   To which glad place, a worthier spirit than I
            Must lead thy steps, if thou desire to come,
            With whom I'll leave thee then, and say good-bye;

124   For the Emperor of that high Imperium
            Wills not that I, once rebel to His crown,
            Into that city of His should lead men home.

127   Everywhere is His realm, but there His throne,
            There is His city and exalted seat:
            Thrice-blest whom there He chooses for His own!'

130   Then I to him: 'Poet, I thee entreat,
            By that great God whom thou didst never know,
            Lead on, that I may free my wandering feet

133   From these snares and from worse; and I will go
            Along with thee, St Peter's Gate to find,
            And those whom thou portray'st as suffering so.'

136   So he moved on; and I moved on behind.

THE IMAGES. *The Dark Wood* is the image of Sin or Error —
not so much of any specific act of sin or intellectual
perversion as of that spritual condition called 'hardness of
heart', in which sinfulness has so taken possession of the

6

soul as to render it incapable of turning to God, or even knowing which way to turn.

The Mountain, which on the mystical level is the image of the Soul's Ascent to God, is thus on the moral level the image of Repentance, by which the sinner returns to God. It can be ascended directly from 'the right road', but not from the Dark Wood, because there the soul's cherished sins have become, as it were, externalized, and appear to it like demons or 'beasts' with a will and power of their own, blocking all progress. Once lost in the Dark Wood, a man can only escape by so descending into himself that he sees his sins, not as an external obstacle, but as the will to chaos and death within him (Hell). Only when he has 'died to sin' can he repent and purge it. Mount Purgatory and the Mountain of Canto I are, therefore, really one and the same mountain, as seen on the far side, and on this side, of the 'death unto sin'.

The Beasts. These are the images of sin. They may be identified with Lust, Pride, and Avarice respectively, or with the sins of Youth, Manhood, and Age; but they are perhaps best thought of as the images of the three *types* of sin which, if not repented, land the soul in one or other of the three main divisions of Hell.

The gay *Leopard* is the image of the self-indulgent sins – *Incontinence*; the fierce *Lion*, of the violent sins – *Bestiality*; the *She-Wolf* of the malicious sins, which involve *Fraud*.

The Greyhound has been much argued about. I think it has both a historical and a spiritual significance. Historically, it is perhaps the image of some hoped-for political saviour who should establish the just World-Empire. Spiritually, the Greyhound, which has the attributes of God ('wisdom, love and power'), is probably the image of the reign of the Holy Ghost on earth – the visible Kingdom of God for which we pray in the Lord's Prayer.

NOTES. l. 1: *midway*: i.e. at the age of 35, the middle point of man's earthly pilgrimage of three-score and ten years.

l. 17: *that planet bright*: the Sun. In medieval astronomy, the Earth was looked upon as being the centre of the universe, and the sun counted as a planet. In the *Comedy*, the Sun is often used as a figure for 'the spiritual sun, which is God'.

l. 27: *whence no man yet came ever out alive*: Dante is by no means 'out' as yet; nor will he be, until he has passed through the 'death unto sin'.

l. 30: *so that the fixed foot always was the lower*: i.e. he was going uphill. In walking, there is always one fixed foot and one moving foot; in going uphill, the moving foot is brought *above*, and in going downhill *below*, the fixed foot.

l. 37: *in his native sign*: According to tradition, the Sun was in the Zodiacal sign of Aries (the Ram) at the moment of the creation. The Sun is in Aries from 21 March to 21 April: therefore the 'sweet season' is that of spring. Later, we shall discover that the day is Good Friday, and that the moon was full on the previous night. These indications do not precisely correspond to the actual Easter sky of 1300; Dante has merely described the astronomical phenomena typical of Eastertide.

ll. 63–4: *as though grown voiceless from long lack of speech*: i.e. the form is trying to speak to Dante, but cannot make itself heard. From the point of view of the *story*, I think this means that, being in fact that of a ghost, it cannot speak until Dante has established communication by addressing it first. *Allegorically*, we may take it in two ways: (1) on the historical level, it perhaps means that the wisdom and poetry of the classical age had been long neglected; (2) on the spiritual level, it undoubtedly means that Dante had sunk so deep into sin that the voice of reason, and even of poetry itself, had become faint and almost powerless to recall him.

l. 70: *sub Julio*: under Julius (Caesar). Virgil was born in 70 B.C. and had published none of his great poems before the murder of Julius in 44 B.C., so that he never enjoyed his patronage.

l. 87: *the noble style*: Dante, in 1300, was already a poet of considerable reputation for his love-lyrics and philosophic odes, though he had not as yet composed any narrative verse directly modelled upon the *Aeneid*. When he says that he owes to Virgil the '*bello stilo* which has won him honour', he can scarcely be referring to the style of his own *prose* works, whether in Latin or Italian, still less to that of the as yet unwritten *Comedy*. Presumably he means that he had studied to imitate, in his poems written in the vernacular, the elegance, concise power, and melodious rhythms of the Virgilian line.

l. 105: *between Feltro and Feltro*: This is a much-debated line. If the Greyhound represents a political 'saviour', it may mean that his birthplace lies between Feltre in Venetia and Montefeltro in Romagna (i.e. in the valley of the Po). But some commentators think that 'feltro' is not a geographical

9

name at all, but simply that of a coarse cloth (felt, or frieze); in which case Dante would be expecting salvation to come from among those who wear the robe of poverty, and have renounced 'gold and ground' – i.e. earthly possessions. We should perhaps translate: 'In cloth of frieze his people shall be found.'

l. 106: *low Italy*: The Italian word is *umile*, humble, which may mean either 'low-lying', as opposed to 'high Italy' among the Alps, or 'humiliated', with reference to the degradation to which the country had been brought. In either case, the classical allusions which follow show that Dante meant Rome.

l. 114: *an eternal place and terrible*: Hell.

l. 117: *the second death*: this might mean 'cry for a second death to put an end to their misery', but more probably means 'cry out because of the pains of hell', in allusion to *Rev.* xx. 14.

ll. 118–19: *those who in the fire are happy*: the redeemed in Purgatory.

l. 134: *St Peter's Gate*: the gate by which redeemed souls are admitted to Purgatory; not the gate of Heaven.

Canto II

THE STORY. *Dante's attempts to climb the Mountain have taken the whole day and it is now Good Friday evening. Dante has not gone far before he loses heart and 'begins to make excuse'. To his specious arguments Virgil replies flatly: 'This is mere cowardice;' and then tells how Beatrice, prompted by St Lucy at the instance of the Virgin Mary herself, descended into Limbo to entreat him to go to Dante's rescue. Thus encouraged, Dante pulls himself together, and they start off again.*

Day was departing and the dusk drew on,
    Loosing from labour every living thing
    Save me, in all the world; I – I alone –

Must gird me to the wars – rough travelling,   4
    And pity's sharp assault upon the heart –
    Which memory shall record, unfaltering;

Now, Muses, now, high Genius, do your part!   7
    And Memory, faithful scrivener to the eyes,
    Here show thy virtue, noble as thou art!

I soon began: 'Poet – dear guide – 'twere wise   10
    Surely, to test my powers and weigh their worth
    Ere trusting me to this great enterprise.

13   Thou sayest, the author of young Silvius' birth,
        Did to the world immortal, mortal go,
        Clothed in the body of flesh he wore on earth –

16   Granted; if Hell's great Foeman deigned to show
        To *him* such favour, seeing the vast effect,
        And what and who his destined issue – no,

19   That need surprise no thoughtful intellect,
        Since to Rome's fostering city and empery
        High Heaven had sealed him as the father-elect;

22   Both these were there established, verily,
        To found that place, holy and dedicate,
        Wherein great Peter's heir should hold his See;

25   So that the deed thy verses celebrate
        Taught him the road to victory, and bestowed
        The Papal Mantle in its high estate.

28   Thither the Chosen Vessel, in like mode,
        Went afterward, and much confirmed thereby
        The faith that sets us on salvation's road.

31   But how should *I* go there? Who says so? Why?
        I'm not Aeneas, and I am not Paul!
        Who thinks me fit? Not others. And not I.

34   Say I submit, and go – suppose I fall
        Into some folly? Though I speak but ill,
        Thy better wisdom will construe it all.'

37   As one who wills, and then unwills his will,
        Changing his mind with every changing whim,
        Till all his best intentions come to nil,

So I stood havering in that moorland dim,   40
   While through fond rifts of fancy oozed away
   The first quick zest that filled me to the brim.

'If I have grasped what thou dost seem to say,'   43
   The shade of greatness answered, 'these doubts breed
   From sheer black cowardice, which day by day

Lays ambushes for men, checking the speed   46
   Of honourable purpose in mid-flight,
   As shapes half-seen startle a shying steed.

Well then, to rid thee of this foolish fright,   49
   Hear why I came, and learn whose eloquence
   Urged me to take compassion on thy plight.

While I was with the spirits who dwell suspense,   52
   A Lady summoned me – so blest, so rare,
   I begged her to command my diligence.

Her eyes outshone the firmament by far   55
   As she began, in her own gracious tongue,
   Gentle and low, as tongues of angels are:

"O courteous Mantuan soul, whose skill in song   58
   Keeps green on earth a fame that shall not end
   While motion rolls the turning spheres along!

A friend of mine, who is not Fortune's friend,   61
   Is hard beset upon the shadowy coast;
   Terrors and snares his fearful steps attend,

Driving him back; yea, and I fear almost   64
   I have risen too late to help – for I was told
   Such news of him in Heaven – he's too far lost.

67 But thou – go thou! Lift up thy voice of gold;
        Try every needful means to find and reach
        And free him, that my heart may rest consoled.

70 Beatrice am I, who thy good speed beseech;
        Love that first moved me from the blissful place
        Whither I'd fain return, now moves my speech.

73 Lo! when I stand before my Lord's bright face
        I'll praise thee many a time to Him." Thereon
        She fell on silence; I replied apace:

76 "Excellent lady, for whose sake alone
        The breed of men exceeds all things that dwell
        Closed in the heaven whose circles narrowest run

79 To do thy bidding pleases me so well
        That were't already done, I should seem slow;
        I know thy wish, and more needs not to tell.

82 Yet say – how can thy blest feet bear to know
        This dark road downward to the dreadful centre,
        From that wide room which thou dost yearn for so?"

85 "Few words will serve (if thou desire to enter
        Thus far into our mystery)," she said,
        "To tell thee why I have no fear to venture.

88 Of hurtful things we ought to be afraid,
        But of no others, truly, inasmuch
        As these have nothing to give cause for dread;

91 My nature, by God's mercy, is made such
        As your calamities can nowise shake,
        Nor these dark fires have any power to touch.

Heaven hath a noble Lady, who doth take   94
  Ruth of this man thou goest to disensnare
  Such that high doom is cancelled for her sake.

She summoned Lucy to her side, and there   97
  Exhorted her: 'Thy faithful votary
  Needs thee, and I commend him to thy care.'

Lucy, the foe to every cruelty,   100
  Ran quickly and came and found me in my place
  Beside ancestral Rachel, crying to me:

'How now, how now, Beatrice, God's true praise!   103
  No help for him who once thy liegeman was,
  Quitting the common herd to win thy grace?

Dost thou not hear his piteous cries, alas?   106
  Dost thou not see death grapple him, on the river
  Whose furious rage no ocean can surpass?'

When I heard that, no living wight was ever   109
  So swift to seek his good or flee his fear
  As I from that high resting-place to sever

And speed me down, trusting my purpose dear   112
  To thee, and to thy golden rhetoric
  Which honours thee, and honours all who hear."

She spoke; and as she turned from me the quick   115
  Tears starred the lustre of her eyes, which still
  Spurred on my going with a keener prick.

Therefore I sought thee out, as was her will,   118
  And brought thee safe off from that beast of prey
  Which barred thee from the short road up the hill.

121 What ails thee then? Why, why this dull delay?
　　Why bring so white a liver to the deed?
　　Why canst thou find no manhood to display

124 When three such blessed ladies deign to plead
　　Thy cause at that supreme assize of right,
　　And when my words promise thee such good speed?'

127 As little flowers, which all the frosty night
　　Hung pinched and drooping, lift their stalks and fan
　　Their blossoms out, touched by the warm white light,

130 So did my fainting powers; and therewith ran
　　Such good, strong courage round about my heart
　　That I spoke boldly out like a free man:

133 'O blessed she that stooped to take my part!
　　O courteous thou, to obey her true-discerning
　　Speech, and thus promptly to my rescue start!

136 Fired by thy words, my spirit now is burning
　　So to go on, and see this venture through.
　　I find my former stout resolve returning.

139 Forward! henceforth there's but one will for two,
　　Thou master, and thou leader, and thou lord.'
　　I spoke; he moved; so, setting out anew,

142 I entered on that savage path and forward.

THE IMAGES. *Mary, The Blessed Virgin*, whom the Church
calls *Theotokos* (Mother of God), is the historical and

16

universal God-bearer, of whom Beatrice, like any other God-bearing image, is a particular type. Mary is thus, in an especial and supreme manner, the vessel of Divine Grace, as experienced in, and mediated through, the redeemed creation. (Note that the name of Mary, like the name of Christ, is never spoken in Hell.)

Lucìa (St Lucy), a virgin martyr of the third century, is the patron saint of those with weak sight, and chosen here as the image of Illuminating Grace. Mary, Beatrice, and Lucìa are a threefold image of Divine Grace in its various manifestations.

Virgil's Mission. Dante is so far gone in sin and error that Divine Grace can no longer move him directly; but there is still something left in him which is capable of responding to the voice of poetry and of human reason; and this, under Grace, may yet be used to lead him back to God. In this profound and beautiful image, Dante places Religion, on the one hand, and human Art and Philosophy, on the other, in their just relationship.

NOTES. l. 7: Canto I forms, as it were, a prologue to the whole *Divine Comedy*. The actual *Inferno* (Hell) begins with Canto II; and here we have the invocation which, in each of the three books, prefaces the journey to Hell, Purgatory, and Paradise respectively. It is addressed, in the classic manner, to the Muses, to Genius, and to Memory, the Mother of the Muses. (As the story proceeds, Dante invokes higher, and still higher aid; till the final invocation, towards the end of the *Paradiso*, is made to God, the 'supreme light' Himself.)

l. 13: *the author of young Silvius' birth*: Aeneas; the allusion is to the sixth book of the *Aeneid*, which describes how Aeneas visits Hades and is told that he is to settle in Italy and so bring about the foundation of Rome, the seat both of the Empire and of the Papacy.

l. 16: *Hell's great Foeman*: God.

l. 28: *the Chosen Vessel*: St Paul (*Acts* IX. 15). His vision of Hell is described in the fourth-century apocryphal book known as *The Apocalypse of Paul*, which Dante had evidently read. There is probably also an allusion to 2 *Cor.* XII. 2.

l. 52: *the spirits who dwell suspense*: Those of the virtuous pagans, who taste neither the bliss of salvation nor the pains of damnation, but dwell forever suspended between the two, in Limbo, the uppermost circle of Hell. (We shall meet them in Canto IV.)

l. 78: *the heaven whose circles narrowest run*: The heaven of the Moon, the smallest and nearest to the Earth.

l. 91: *my nature, by God's mercy, is made such*: The souls of the blessed can still pity the self-inflicted misery of the wicked, but they can no longer be hurt or infected by it.

l. 102: *ancestral Rachel*: Leah and Rachel, the two wives of Jacob, figure respectively the active and the contemplative life.

l. 107: *the river*: No literal river is intended; it is only a metaphor for human life.

l. 120: *the short road up the hill*: This line shows clearly that the 'blissful Mountain' and Mount Purgatory are in reality one and the same; since the Beasts prevent Dante from taking 'the short road', he is obliged to go by the long road – i.e. through Hell – to find the mountain again on the other side of the world.

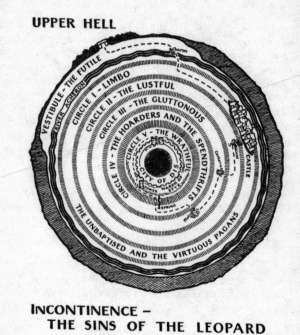

UPPER HELL

**INCONTINENCE –
THE SINS OF THE LEOPARD**

Canto III

THE STORY. *Arriving at the gate of Hell, the Poets read the inscription upon its lintel. They enter and find themselves in the Vestibule of Hell, where the Futile run perpetually after a whirling standard. Passing quickly on, they reach the river Acheron. Here the souls of all the damned come at death to be ferried across by Charon, who refuses to take the living body of Dante till Virgil silences him with a word of power. While they are watching the departure of a boatload of souls the river banks are shaken by an earthquake so violent that Dante swoons away.*

THROUGH ME THE ROAD TO THE CITY OF DESOLATION,
   THROUGH ME THE ROAD TO SORROWS DIUTURNAL,
   THROUGH ME THE ROAD AMONG THE LOST CREATION.

JUSTICE MOVED MY GREAT MAKER; GOD ETERNAL   4
   WROUGHT ME: THE POWER, AND THE UNSEARCHABLY
   HIGH WISDOM, AND THE PRIMAL LOVE SUPERNAL.

NOTHING ERE I WAS MADE WAS MADE TO BE   7
   SAVE THINGS ETERNE, AND I ETERNE ABIDE;
   LAY DOWN ALL HOPE, YOU THAT GO IN BY ME.

These words, of sombre colour, I descried   10
   Writ on the lintel of a gateway; 'Sir,
   This sentence is right hard for me,' I cried.

21

13 And like a man of quick discernment: 'Here
        Lay down all thy distrust,' said he, 'reject
        Dead from within thee every coward fear;

16 We've reached the place I told thee to expect,
        Where thou shouldst see the miserable race,
        Those who have lost the good of intellect.'

19 He laid his hand on mine, and with a face
        So joyous that it comforted my quailing,
        Into the hidden things he led my ways.

22 Here sighing, and here crying, and loud railing
        Smote on the starless air, with lamentation,
        So that at first I wept to hear such wailing.

25 Tongues mixed and mingled, horrible execration,
        Shrill shrieks, hoarse groans, fierce yells and hideous blether
        And clapping of hands thereto, without cessation

28 Made tumult through the timeless night, that hither
        And thither drives in dizzying circles sped,
        As whirlwind whips the spinning sands together.

31 Whereat, with horror flapping round my head:
        'Master, what's this I hear? Who can they be,
        These people so distraught with grief?' I said.

34 And he replied: 'The dismal company
        Of wretched spirits thus find their guerdon due
        Whose lives knew neither praise nor infamy;

37 They're mingled with that caitiff angle-crew
        Who against God rebelled not, nor to Him
        Were faithful, but to self alone were true;

22

Heaven cast them forth – their presence there would dim   40
  The light; deep Hell rejects so base a herd,
  Lest sin should boast itself because of them.'

Then I: 'But, Master, by what torment spurred   43
  Are they driven on to vent such bitter breath?'
  He answered: 'I will tell thee in a word:

This dreary huddle has no hope of death,   46
  Yet its blind life trails on so low and crass
  That every other fate it envieth.

No reputation in the world it has,   49
  Mercy and doom hold it alike in scorn –
  Let us not speak of these; but look, and pass.'

So I beheld, and lo! an ensign borne   52
  Whirling, that span and ran, as in disdain
  Of any rest; and there the folk forlorn

Rushed after it, in such an endless train,   55
  It never would have entered in my head
  There were so many men whom death had slain.

And when I'd noted here and there a shade   58
  Whose face I knew, I saw and recognized
  The coward spirit of the man who made

The great refusal; and that proof sufficed;   61
  Here was that rabble, here without a doubt,
  Whom God and whom His enemies despised.

This scum, who'd never lived, now fled about   64
  Naked and goaded, for a swarm of fierce
  Hornets and wasps stung all the wretched rout

67   Until their cheeks ran blood, whose slubbered smears,
      Mingled with brine, around their footsteps fell,
      Where loathly worms licked up their blood and tears.

70   Then I peered on ahead, and soon quite well
      Made out the hither bank of a wide stream,
      Where stood much people. 'Sir,' said I, 'pray tell

73   Who these are, what their custom, why they seem
      So eager to pass over and be gone –
      If I may trust my sight in this pale gleam.'

76   And he to me: 'The whole shall be made known;
      Only have patience till we stay our feet
      On yonder sorrowful shore of Acheron.'

79   Abashed, I dropped my eyes; and, lest unmeet
      Chatter should vex him, held my tongue, and so
      Paced on with him, in silence and discreet,

82   To the riverside. When from the far bank lo!
      A boat shot forth, whose white-haired boatman old
      Bawled as he came: 'Woe to the wicked! Woe!

85   Never you hope to look on Heaven – behold!
      I come to ferry you hence across the tide
      To endless night, fierce fires and shramming cold.

88   And thou, the living man there! stand aside
      From these who are dead!' I budged not, but abode;
      So, when he saw me hold my ground, he cried:

91   'Away with thee! for by another road
      And other ferries thou shalt make the shore,
      Not here; a lighter skiff must bear thy load.'

Then said my guide: 'Charon, why wilt thou roar   94
    And chafe in vain? Thus it is willed where power
    And will are one; enough; ask thou no more.'

This shut the shaggy mouth up of that sour   97
    Infernal ferryman of the livid wash,
    Only his flame-ringed eyeballs rolled a-glower.

But those outwearied, naked souls – how gash   100
    And pale they grew, chattering their teeth for dread,
    When first they felt his harsh tongue's cruel lash.

God they blaspheme, blaspheme their parents' bed,   103
    The human race, the place, the time, the blood,
    The seed that got them, and the womb that bred;

Then, huddling hugger-mugger, down they scud,   106
    Dismally wailing, to the accursed strand
    Which waits for every man that fears not God.

Charon, his eyes red like a burning brand,   109
    Thumps with his oar the lingerers that delay,
    And rounds them up, and beckons with his hand.

And as, by one and one, leaves drift away   112
    In autumn, till the bough from which they fall
    Sees the earth strewn with all its brave array,

So, from the bank there, one by one, drop all   115
    Adam's ill seed, when signalled off the mark,
    As drops the falcon to the falconer's call.

Away they're borne across the waters dark,   118
    And ere they land that side the stream, anon
    Fresh troops this side come flocking to embark.

121   Then said my courteous master: 'See, my son,
       All those that die beneath God's righteous ire
       From every country come here every one.

124   They press to pass the river, for the fire
       Of heavenly justice stings and spurs them so
       That all their fear is changed into desire;

127   And by this passage, good souls never go;
       Therefore, if Charon chide thee, do thou look
       What this may mean – 'tis not so hard to know.'

130   When he thus said, the dusky champaign shook
       So terribly that, thinking on the event,
       I feel the sweat pour off me like a brook.

133   The sodden ground belched wind, and through the rent
       Shot the red levin, with a flash and sweep
       That robbed me of my wits, incontinent;

136   And down I fell, as one that swoons on sleep.

THE IMAGES. *Hell-Gate.* High and wide and without bars, the door 'whose threshold is denied to none' always waits to receive those who are astray in the Dark Wood. Anyone may enter if he so chooses, but if he does, he must abandon hope, since it leads nowhere but to the *Città Dolente*, the City of Desolation. In the *story*, Hell is filled with the souls of those who died with their wills set to enter by that gate; in the *allegory*, these souls are the images of sin in the self or in society.

The Vestibule was presumably suggested to Dante by the description in *Aeneid* VI (where, however, it is tenanted by rather a different set of people). It does not, I think, occur in any previous Christian eschatology. Heaven and Hell being states in which choice is permanently fixed, there must also be a state in which the refusal of choice is itself fixed, since to refuse choice is in fact to choose indecision. The Vestibule is the abode of the weather-cock mind, the vague tolerance which will neither approve nor condemn, the cautious cowardice for which no decision is ever final. The spirits rush aimlessly after the aimlessly whirling banner, stung and goaded, as of old, by the thought that, in doing anything definite whatsoever, they are missing doing something else.

Acheron, 'the joyless', first of the great rivers of Hell whose names Dante took from Virgil and Virgil from Homer.

Charon, the classical ferryman of the dead. Most of the monstrous organisms by which the functions of Hell are discharged are taken from Greek and Roman mythology. They are neither devils nor damned souls, but the images of perverted appetites, presiding over the circles appropriate to their natures.

NOTES. l. 1: *the City of Desolation* (*la Città Dolente*; lit.: the sorrowful city). Hell, like Heaven, is represented under the figure sometimes of a city, and sometimes of an empire.

ll. 5–6: *power . . . high wisdom . . . primal love*: the attributes of the Trinity.

27

l. 8: *things eterne*: Dante tells how Hell was made when Satan fell from Heaven: it was created 'for the devil and his angels' (*Matt.* XXV. 41) and before it nothing was made except the 'eternal things', i.e. the Angels and the Heavens.

l. 9: *lay down all hope*: For the soul that literally enters Hell there is no return, nor any passage to Purgatory and repentance. Dante is naturally disturbed (l. 12) by this warning. But what he is entering upon, while yet in this life, is not Hell but the vision of Hell, and for him there is a way out, provided he keeps his hope and faith. Accordingly, Virgil enjoins him (ll. 14–15) to reject doubt and fear.

l. 18: *the good of intellect*: In the *Convivio* Dante quotes Aristotle as saying: 'truth is the good of the intellect'. What the lost souls have lost is not the intellect itself, which still functions mechanically, but the *good* of the intellect: i.e. the knowledge of God, who is Truth. (For Dante, as for Aquinas, 'intellect' does not mean what we call, colloquially, 'braininess'; it means the whole 'reasonable soul' of man.)

l. 61: *the great refusal*: Probably Celestine V, who, in 1294, at the age of 80, was made pope, but resigned the papacy five months later. His successor was Pope Boniface VIII, to whom Dante attributed many of the evils which had overtaken the Church.

ll. 91–2: *another road and other ferries*: Souls destined for Heaven never cross Acheron; they assemble at the mouth of the Tiber and are taken in a boat piloted by an angel to Mount Purgatory at the Antipodes. Charon recognizes that Dante is a soul in Grace. (See ll. 127–9.)

l. 126: *all their fear is changed into desire*: This is another of the important passages in which Dante emphasizes that Hell is the soul's choice. The damned fear it and long for it, as in this life a man may hate the sin which makes him miserable, and yet obstinately seek and wallow in it.

Canto IV

THE STORY. *Recovering from his swoon, Dante finds himself across Acheron and on the edge of the actual Pit of Hell. He follows Virgil into the First Circle – the Limbo where the Unbaptized and the Virtuous Pagans dwell 'suspended', knowing no torment save exclusion from the positive bliss of God's presence. Virgil tells him of Christ's Harrowing of Hell, and then shows him the habitation of the great men of antiquity – poets, heroes, and philosophers.*

A heavy peel of thunder came to waken me
   Out of the stunning slumber that had bound me,
   Startling me up as though rude hands had shaken me.

4   I rose, and cast my rested eyes around me,
      Gazing intent to satisfy my wonder
      Concerning the strange place wherein I found me.

7   Hear truth: I stood on the steep brink whereunder
      Runs down the dolorous chasm of the Pit,
      Ringing with infinite groans like gathered thunder.

10   Deep, dense, and by no faintest glimmer lit
      It lay, and though I strained my sight to find
      Bottom, not one thing could I see in it.

13   'Down must we go, to that dark world and blind,'
      The poet said, turning on me a bleak
      Blanched face; 'I will go first – come thou behind.'

Then I, who had marked the colour of his cheek: 16
    'How can I go, when even thou art white
    For fear, who art wont to cheer me when I'm weak?'

But he: 'Not so; the anguish infinite   19
    They suffer yonder paints my countenance
    With pity, which thou takest for affright;

Come, we have far to go; let us advance.'   22
    So, entering, he made me enter, where
    The Pit's first circle makes circumference.

We heard no loud complaint, no crying there,   25
    No sound of grief except the sound of sighing
    Quivering for ever through the eternal air;

Grief, not for torment, but for loss undying,   28
    By women, men, and children sighed for so,
    Sorrowers thick-thronged, their sorrows multiplying.

Then my good guide: 'Thou dost not ask me who   31
    These spirits are,' said he, 'whom thou perceivest?
    Ere going further, I would have thee know

They sinned not; yet their merit lacked its chiefest   34
    Fulfilment, lacking baptism, which is
    The gateway to the faith which thou believest;

Or, living before Christendom, their knees   37
    Paid not aright those tributes that belong
    To God; and I myself am one of these.

For such defects alone – no other wrong –   40
    We are lost; yet only by this grief offended:
    That, without hope, we ever live, and long.'

43   Grief smote my heart to think, as he thus ended,
          What souls I knew, of great and soveran
          Virtue, who in that Limbo dwelt suspended.

46   'Tell me, sir – tell me, Master,' I began
          (In hope some fresh assurance to be gleaning
          Of our sin-conquering Faith), 'did any man

49   By his self-merit, or on another leaning,
          Ever fare forth from hence and come to be
          Among the blest?' He took my hidden meaning.

52   'When I was newly in this state,' said he,
          'I saw One come in majesty and awe,
          And on His head were crowns of victory.

55   Our great first father's spirit He did withdraw,
          And righteous Abel, Noah who built the ark,
          Moses who gave and who obeyed the Law,

58   King David, Abraham the Patriarch,
          Israel with his father and generation,
          Rachel, for whom he did such deeds of mark,

61   With many another of His chosen nation;
          These did He bless; and know, that ere that day
          No human soul had ever seen salvation.'

64   While he thus spake, we still made no delay,
          But passed the wood – I mean, the wood (as 'twere)
          Of souls ranged thick as trees. Being now some way –

67   Not far – from where I'd slept, I saw appear
          A light, which overcame the shadowy face
          Of gloom, and made a glowing hemisphere.

'Twas yet some distance on, yet I could trace 70
  So much as brought conviction to my heart
  That persons of great honour held that place.

'O thou that honour'st every science and art, 73
  Say, who are these whose honour gives them claim
  To different customs and a sphere apart?'

And he to me: 'Their honourable name, 76
  Still in thy world resounding as it does,
  Wins here from Heaven the favour due to fame.'

Meanwhile I heard a voice that cried out thus: 79
  'Honour the most high poet! his great shade,
  Which was departed, is returned to us.'

It paused there, and was still; and lo! there made 82
  Toward us, four mighty shadows of the dead,
  Who in their mien nor grief nor joy displayed.

'Mark well the first of these,' my master said, 85
  'Who in his right hand bears a naked sword
  And goes before the three as chief and head;

Homer is he, the poets' sovran lord; 88
  Next, Horace comes, the keen satirical;
  Ovid the third; and Lucan afterward.

Because I share with these that honourable 91
  Grand title the sole voice was heard to cry
  They do me honour, and therein do well.'

Thus in their school assembled I, even I, 94
  Looked on the lords of loftiest song, whose style
  O'er all the rest goes soaring eagle-high.

97 When they had talked together a short while
        They all with signs of welcome turned my way,
        Which moved my master to a kindly smile;

100 And greater honour yet they did me – yea,
        Into their fellowship they deigned invite
        And make me sixth among such minds as they.

103 So we moved slowly onward toward the light
        In talk 'twere as unfitting to repeat
        Here, as to speak there was both fit and right.

106 And presently we reached a noble seat –
        A castle, girt with seven high walls around,
        And moated with a goodly rivulet

109 O'er which we went as though upon dry ground;
        With those wise men I passed the sevenfold gate
        Into a fresh green meadow, where we found

112 Persons with grave and tranquil eyes, and great
        Authority in their carriage and attitude,
        Who spoke but seldom and in voice sedate.

115 So here we walked aside a little, and stood
        Upon an open eminence, lit serene
        And clear, whence one and all might well be viewed.

118 Plain in my sight on the enamelled green
        All those grand spirits were shown me one by one –
        It thrills my heart to think what I have seen!

121 I saw Electra, saw with her anon
        Hector, Aeneas, many a Trojan peer,
        And hawk-eyed Caesar in his habergeon;

I saw Camilla and bold Penthesilea,   124
     On the other hand; Latinus on his throne
     Beside Lavinia his daughter dear;

Brutus, by whom proud Tarquin was o'erthrown,   127
     Marcia, Cornelia, Julia, Lucrece – and
     I saw great Saladin, aloof, alone.

Higher I raised my brows and further scanned,   130
     And saw the Master of the men who know
     Seated amid the philosophic band;

All do him honour and deep reverence show;   133
     Socrates, Plato, in the nearest room
     To him; Diogenes, Thales and Zeno,

Democritus, who held that all things come   136
     By chance; Empedocles, Anaxagoras wise,
     And Heraclitus, him that wept for doom;

Dioscorides, who named the qualities,   139
     Tully and Orpheus, Linus, and thereby
     Good Seneca, well-skilled to moralize;

Euclid the geometrician, Ptolemy,   142
     Galen, Hippocrates, and Avicen,
     Averrhoës who made the commentary –

Nay, but I tell not all that I saw then;   145
     The long theme drives me hard, and every
          where
     The wondrous truth outstrips my staggering
          pen.

The group of six dwindles to two; we fare
         Forth a new way, I and my guide withal,
         Out from that quiet to the quivering air,

And reach a place where nothing shines at all.

THE IMAGES. After those who refused choice come those
   without opportunity of choice. They could not, that is,
   choose Christ; they could, and did, choose human virtue,
   and for that they have their reward. (Pagans who chose
   evil by their own standards are judged by these standards –
   cf. *Rom.* II. 8–15 – and are found lower down.) Here again,
   the souls 'have what they chose'; they enjoy that kind of
   after-life which they themselves imagined for the virtuous
   dead; their failure lay in not imagining better. They are
   lost because they 'had not faith' – primarily the Christian
   Faith, but also, more generally, faith in the nature of
   things. The *allegory* is clear: it is the weakness of Human-
   ism to fall short in the imagination of ecstasy; at its best it
   is noble, reasonable, and cold, and however optimistic
   about a balanced happiness in this world, pessimistic about
   a rapturous eternity. Sometimes wistfully aware that others
   claim the experience of this positive bliss, the Humanist
   can neither accept it by faith, embrace it by hope, nor
   abandon himself to it in charity.

NOTES. l. 7: *I stood on the steep brink*: It is disputed how
   Dante passed Acheron; the simplest explanation is that
   Charon, obedient to Virgil's 'word of power', ferried him

across during his swoon. Technically speaking, Dante had to describe a passage by boat in Canto VIII, and did not want to anticipate his effects; I think, however, he had also an allegorical reason for omitting the description here. Note that the 'peal of thunder' in l. 1 is not that which followed the lightning-flash at the end of Canto III, but (l. 9) the din issuing from the mouth of the Pit – an orchestra of discord, here blended into one confused roar, which, resolved into its component disharmonies, will accompany us to the bottom circle of Hell.

l. 53: *I saw One come*: The episode, based upon I *Peter* III. 19, of Christ's descent into Limbo to rescue the souls of the patriarchs (the 'Harrowing of Hell') was a favourite subject of medieval legend and drama. The crucifixion is reckoned as having occurred in A.D. 34, when Virgil had been dead 53 years. Note that the name of Christ is never spoken in Hell – He is always referred to by some periphrasis.

l. 55: *our great first father*: Adam.

l. 106: *a noble seat*: The scene is, I think, a medievalized version of the Elysian Fields, surrounded by 'many-watered Eridanus'. (*Aeneid* VI. 659). Detailed allegorical interpretations of the seven gates, walls, etc., have no great value.

l. 121: *Electra, etc.*: Pride of place is given to the Trojans, founders of the Roman line; (Julius) Caesar is grouped with them as a descendant of Aeneas.

l. 129: *Saladin*: His inclusion here, along with Lucan, Averrhoës, and other A.D. personages who were not, strictly speaking, without opportunity of choice, perhaps tacitly indicates Dante's opinion about all those who, though living in touch with Christianity and practising all the moral virtues, find themselves sincerely unable to accept the Christian revelation.

l. 131: *the Master of the men who know*: Aristotle.

Canto V

THE STORY. *Dante and Virgil descend from the First Circle to the Second (the first of the Circles of Incontinence). On the threshold sits Minos, the judge of Hell, assigning the souls to their appropriate places of torment. His opposition is overcome by Virgil's word of power, and the Poets enter the Circle, where the souls of the Lustful are tossed for ever upon a howling wind. After Virgil has pointed out a number of famous lovers, Dante speaks to the shade of Francesca da Rimini, who tells him her story.*

From the first circle thus I came descending
    To the second, which, in narrower compass turning,
    Holds greater woe, with outcry loud and rending.

There in the threshold, horrible and girning,   4
    Grim Minos sits, holding his ghastly session,
    And, as he girds him, sentencing and spurning;

For when the ill soul faces him, confession   7
    Pours out of it till nothing's left to tell;
    Whereon that connoisseur of all transgression

Assigns it to its proper place in hell,   10
    As many grades as he would have it fall,
    So oft he belts him round with his own tail.

13   Before him stands a throng continual;
        Each comes in turn to abye the fell arraign;
        They speak – they hear – they're whirled down one and all.

16   'Ho! thou that comest to the house of pain,'
        Cried Minos when he saw me, the appliance
        Of his dread powers suspending, 'think again

19   How thou dost go, in whom is thy reliance;
        Be not deceived by the wide open door!'
        Then said my guide: 'Wherefore this loud defiance?

22   Hinder not thou his fated way; be sure
        Hindrance is vain; thus it is willed where will
        And power are one; enough; ask thou no more.'

25   And now the sounds of grief begin to fill
        My ear; I'm come where cries of anguish smite
        My shrinking sense, and lamentation shrill –

28   A place made dumb of every glimmer of light,
        Which bellows like tempestuous ocean birling
        In the batter of a two-way wind's buffet and fight.

31   The blast of hell that never rests from whirling
        Harries the spirits along in the sweep of its swath,
        And vexes them, for ever beating and hurling.

34   When they are borne to the rim of the ruinous path
        With cry and wail and shriek they are caught by the gust,
        Railing and cursing the power of the Lord's wrath.

37   Into this torment carnal sinners are thrust,
        So I was told – the sinners who make their reason
        Bond thrall under the yoke of their lust.

Like as the starlings wheel in the wintry season 40
  In wide and clustering flocks wing-borne, wind-borne
  Even so they go, the souls who did this treason,

Hither and thither, and up and down, outworn, 43
  Hopeless of any rest – rest, did I say?
  Of the least minishing of their pangs forlorn.

And as the cranes go chanting their harsh lay, 46
  Across the sky in long procession trailing,
  So I beheld some shadows borne my way,

Driven on the blast and uttering wail on wailing; 49
  Wherefore I said: 'O Master, art thou able
  To name these spirits thrashed by the black wind's flailing?'

'Among this band,' said he, 'whose name and fable 52
  Thou seek'st to know, the first who yonder flies
  Was empress of many tongues, mistress of Babel.

She was so broken to lascivious vice 55
  She licensed lust by law, in hopes to cover
  Her scandal of unnumbered harlotries.

This was Semiramis; 'tis written of her 58
  That she was wife to Ninus and heiress, too,
  Who reigned in the land the Soldan now rules over.

Lo! she that slew herself for love, untrue 61
  To Sychaeus' ashes. Lo! tost on the blast,
  Voluptuous Cleopatra, whom love slew.

Look, look on Helen, for whose sake rolled past 64
  Long evil years. See great Achilles yonder,
  Who warred with love, and that war was his last.

67 See Paris, Tristram see!' And many – oh, wonder
   Many – a thousand more, he showed by name
   And pointing hand, whose life love rent asunder.

70 And when I had heard my Doctor tell the fame
   Of all those knights and ladies of long ago,
   I was pierced through with pity, and my head swam.

73 'Poet,' said I, 'fain would I speak those two
   That seem to ride as light as any foam,
   And hand in hand on the dark wind drifting go.'

76 And he replied: 'Wait till they nearer roam,
   And thou shalt see; summon them to thy side
   By the power of the love that leads them, and they will come.'

79 So, as they eddied past on the whirling tide,
   I raised my voice: 'O souls that wearily rove,
   Come to us, speak to us – if it be not denied.'

82 And as desire wafts homeward dove with dove
   To their sweet nest, on raised and steady wing
   Down-dropping through the air, impelled by love,

85 So these from Dido's flock came fluttering
   And dropping toward us down the cruel wind,
   Such power was in my affectionate summoning.

88 'O living creature, gracious and so kind,
   Coming through this black air to visit us,
   Us, who in death the globe incarnadined,

91 Were the world's King our friend and might we thus
   Entreat, we would entreat Him for thy peace,
   That pitiest so our pangs dispiteous!

Hear all thou wilt, and speak as thou shalt please,   94
    And we will gladly speak with thee and hear,
    While the winds cease to howl, as they now cease.

There is a town upon the sea-coast, near   97
    Where Po with all his streams comes down to rest
    In ocean; I was born and nurtured there.

Love, that so soon takes hold in the gentle breast,   100
    Took this lad with the lovely body they tore
    From me; the way of it leaves me still distrest.

Love, that to no loved heart remits love's score,   103
    Took me with such great joy of him, that see!
    It holds me yet and never shall leave me more.

Love to a single death brought him and me;   106
    Cain's place lies waiting for our murderer now.'
    These words came wafted to us plaintively.

Hearing those wounded souls, I bent my brow   109
    Downward, and thus bemused I let time pass,
    Till the poet said at length: 'What thinkest thou?'

When I could answer, I began: 'Alas!   112
    Sweet thoughts how many, and desire how great,
    Brought down these twain unto the dolorous pass!'

And then I turned to them: 'Thy dreadful fate,   115
    Francesca, makes me weep, it so inspires
    Pity,' said I, 'and grief compassionate.

Tell me – in that time of sighing-sweet desires,   118
    How, and by what, did love his power disclose
    And grant you knowledge of your hidden fires?'

43

121 Then she to me: 'The bitterest woe of woes
   Is to remember in our wretchedness
   Old happy times; and this thy Doctor knows;

124 Yet, if so dear desire thy heart possess
   To know that root of love which wrought our fall,
   I'll be as those who weep and who confess.

127 One day we read for pastime how in thrall
   Lord Lancelot lay to love, who loved the Queen;
   We were alone – we thought no harm at all.

130 As we read on, our eyes met now and then,
   And to our cheeks the changing colour started,
   But just one moment overcame us – when

133 We read of the smile, desired of lips long-thwarted,
   Such smile, by such a lover kissed away,
   He that may never more from me be parted

136 Trembling all over, kissed my mouth. I say
   The book was Galleot, Galleot the complying
   Ribald who wrote; we read no more that day.'

139 While the one spirit thus spoke, the other's crying
   Wailed on me with a sound so lamentable,
   I swooned for pity like as I were dying,

142 And, as a dead man falling, down I fell.

THE IMAGES. *The Circles of Incontinence.* This and the next
three circles are devoted to those who sinned less by

deliberate choice of evil than by failure to make resolute choice of the good. Here are the sins of self-indulgence, weakness of will, and easy yielding to appetite – the 'Sins of the Leopard'.

The Lustful. The image here is sexual, though we need not confine the *allegory* to the sin of unchastity. Lust is a type of *shared* sin; at its best, and so long as it remains a sin of incontinence only, there is mutuality in it and exchange: although, in fact, mutual indulgence only serves to push both parties along the road to Hell, it is not, in intention, wholly selfish. For this reason Dante, with perfect orthodoxy, rates it as the least hateful of the deadly sins. (Sexual sins in which love and mutuality have no part find their place far below.)

Minos, a medievalized version of the classical Judge of the Underworld (see *Aeneid* VI. 432). He may image an accusing conscience. The souls are damned on their own confession, for, Hell being the place of self-knowledge in sin, there can be no more self-deception here. (Similarly, even in the circles of Fraud, all the shades tell Dante the truth about themselves; this is poetically convenient, but, given this conception of Hell, it must be so.) The *literally* damned, having lost 'the good of the intellect', cannot profit by their self-knowledge; *allegorically*, for the living soul, this vision of the Hell in the self is the preliminary to repentance and restoration.

The Black Wind. As the lovers drifted into self-indulgence and were carried away by their passions, so now they drift for ever. The bright, voluptuous sin is now seen *as it is* – a howling darkness of helpless discomfort. (The 'punishment' for sin is simply the sin itself, experienced without illusion – though Dante does not work this out with mathematical rigidity in every circle.)

NOTES. l. 6: *as he girds him, sentencing*: As Dante explains in ll. 11–12, Minos girds himself so many times with his tail to indicate the number of the circle to which each soul is to go.

l. 28: *a place made dumb of every glimmer of light* – (cf. Canto I. 60, 'wherein the sun is mute'): Nevertheless, Dante is able to see the spirits. This is only one of many passages in which the poet conveys to us that the things he perceives during his journey are not perceived altogether by the mortal senses, but after another mode. (In *Purg.* XXI. 29, Virgil explains to another spirit that Dante 'could not come alone, because he does not see after our manner, wherefore I was brought forth from Hell to guide him'). So, in the present case, Dante recognizes that the darkness is total, although he can see in the dark.

l. 61: *she that slew herself for love*: Dido.

l. 88: *O living creature*: The speaker is Francesca da Rimini. Like many of the personages in the *Comedy*, she does not directly name herself, but gives Dante particulars about her birthplace and history which enable him to recognize her. She was the daughter of Guido Vecchio di Polenta of Ravenna, and aunt to Guido Novello di Polenta, who was Dante's friend and host during the latter years of his life; so that her history was of topical interest to Dante's readers. For political reasons, she was married to the deformed Gianciotto, son of Malatesta da Verrucchio, lord of Rimini, but fell in love with his handsome younger brother Paolo, who became her lover. Her husband, having one day surprised them together, stabbed them both to death (1285).

l. 94: *hear all thou wilt*: Tender and beautiful as Dante's handling of Francesca is, he has sketched her with a deadly accuracy. All the good is there; the charm, the courtesy, the instant response to affection, the grateful eagerness to please; but also all the evil; the easy yielding, the inability to say No, the intense self-pity.

l. 97: *a town upon the sea-coast*: Ravenna.

l. 102: *the way of it leaves me still distrest*: Either (1) the way of the murder, because the lovers were killed in the very act of sin and so had no time for repentance; or (2) the way in which their love came about. The story went that Paolo was sent to conduct the marriage negotiations, and that Francesca was tricked into consenting by being led to suppose that he, and not Gianciotto, was to be her bride-groom. In the same way, in the Arthurian romances, Queen Guinevere falls in love with Lancelot when he is sent to woo her on King Arthur's behalf; and it is this parallel which makes the tale of Lancelot so poignant for her and Paolo.

l. 107: *Cain's place*: Caïna, so called after Cain; the first ring of the lowest circle in Hell, where lie those who were treacherous to their own kindred.

l. 123: *thy Doctor*: Virgil (see l. 70). Dante is probably thinking of Aeneas' words to Dido: *infandum, regina, jubes renovare dolorem . . .* (O queen, thou dost bid me renew an unspeakable sorrow . . .), *Aeneid* ii. 3.

l. 137: *the book was Galleot*: In the romance of *Lancelot du Lac*, Galleot (or Galehalt) acted as intermediary between Lancelot and Guinevere, and so in the Middle Ages his name, like that of Pandarus in the tale of *Troilus and Cressida*, became a synonym for a go-between. The sense of the passage is: 'The book was a pander and so was he who wrote it.'

Canto VI

THE STORY. *Dante now finds himself in the Third Circle, where the Gluttonous lie wallowing in the mire, drenched by perpetual rain and mauled by the three-headed dog Cerberus. After Virgil has quieted Cerberus by throwing earth into his jaws, Dante talks to the shade of Ciacco, a Florentine, who prophesies some of the disasters which are about to befall Florence, and tells him where he will find certain other of their fellow-citizens. Virgil tells Dante what the condition of the spirits will be, after the Last Judgment.*

When consciousness returned, which had shut close
    The doors of sense, leaving me stupefied
    For pity of those sad kinsfolk and their woes,

New sufferings and new sufferers, far and wide,   4
    Wher'er I move, or turn myself, or strain
    My curious eyes, are seen on every side.

I am now in the Third Circle: that of rain –   7
    One ceaseless, heavy, cold, accursed quench,
    Whose law and nature vary never a grain;

Huge hailstones, sleet and snow, and turbid drench   10
    Of water sluice down through the darkened air,
    And the soaked earth gives off a putrid stench.

13   Cerberus, the cruel, misshapen monster, there
       Bays in his triple gullet and doglike growls
       Over the wallowing shades; his eyeballs glare

16   A bloodshot crimson, and his bearded jowls
       Are greasy and black; pot-bellied, talon-heeled,
       He clutches and flays and rips and rends the souls.

19   They howl in the rain like hounds; they try to shield
       One flank with the other; with many a twist and squirm,
       The impious wretches writhe in the filthy field.

22   When Cerberus spied us coming, the great Worm,
       He gaped his mouths with all their fangs a-gloat,
       Bristling and quivering till no limb stood firm.

25   At once my guide, spreading both hands wide out,
       Scooped up whole fistfuls of the miry ground
       And shot them swiftly into each craving throat.

28   And as a ravenous and barking hound
       Falls dumb the moment he gets his teeth on food,
       And worries and bolts with never a thought beyond,

31   So did those beastly muzzles of the rude
       Fiend Cerberus, who so yells on the souls, they're all
       Half deafened – or they would be, if they could.

34   Then o'er the shades whom the rain's heavy fall
       Beats down, we forward went; and our feet trod
       Their nothingness, which seems corporeal.

37   These all lay grovelling flat upon the sod;
       Only, as we went by, a single shade
       Sat suddenly up, seeing us pass that road.

'O thou that through this Hell of ours art led,   40
   Look if thou know me, since thou wast, for sure,'
   Said he, 'or ever I was unmade, made.'

Then I to him: 'Perchance thy torments sore   43
   Have changed thee out of knowledge – there's no trusting
   Sight, if I e'er set eyes on thee before.

But say, who art thou? brought by what ill lusting   46
   To such a pass and punishment as, meseems,
   Worse there may be, but nothing so disgusting?'

'Thy native city,' said he, 'where envy teems   49
   And swells so that already it brims the sack,
   Called me her own in the life where the light beams.

Ciacco you citizens nicknamed me – alack!   52
   Damnable gluttony was my soul's disease;
   See how I waste for it now in the rain's wrack.

And I, poor sinner, am not alone: all these   55
   Lie bound in the like penalty with me
   For the like offence.' And there he held his peace,

And I at once began: 'Thy misery   58
   Moves me to tears, Ciacco, and weighs me down.
   But tell me if thou canst, what end may be

In store for the people of our distracted town.   61
   Is there one just man left? And from what source
   To such foul head have these distempers grown?'

And he: 'Long time their strife will run its course,   64
   And come to bloodshed; the wood party thence
   Will drive the other out with brutal force;

67   But within three brief suns their confidence
        Will have a fall, and t'other faction rise
        By help of one who now sits on the fence;

70   And these will lord it long with arrogant eyes,
        Crushing their foes with heavy loads indeed,
        For all their bitter shame and outraged cries.

73   Two righteous men there are, whom none will heed;
        Three sparks from Hell – Avarice, Envy, Pride –
        In all men's bosoms sowed the fiery seed.'

76   His boding speech thus ended; so I cried:
        'Speak on, I beg thee! More, much more reveal!
        Tegghiaio, Farinata – how betide

79   Those worthy men? and Rusticucci's zeal?
        Arrigo, Mosca, and the rest as well
        Whose minds were still set on the public weal?

82   Where are they? Can I find them? Prithee tell –
        I am consumed with my desire to know –
        Feasting in Heaven, or poisoned here in Hell?'

85   He answered: 'With the blacker spirits below,
        Dragged to the depth by other crimes abhorred;
        There shalt thou see them, if so deep thou go.

88   But when to the sweet world thou art restored,
        Recall my name to living memory;
        I'll tell no more, nor speak another word.'

91   Therewith he squinted his straight gaze awry,
        Eyed me awhile, then, dropping down his head,
        Rolled over amid that sightless company.

Then spake my guide: 'He'll rouse no more,' he said,   94
  'Till the last loud angelic trumpet's sounding;
  For when the Enemy Power shall come arrayed

Each soul shall seek its own grave's mournful mounding,   97
  Put on once more its earthly flesh and feature,
  And hear the Doom eternally redounding.'

Thus with slow steps I and my gentle teacher,   100
  Over that filthy sludge of souls and snow,
  Passed on, touching a little upon the nature

Of the life to come. 'Master,' said I, 'this woe –   103
  Will it grow less, or still more fiercely burning
  With the Great Sentence, or remain just so?'

'Go to,' said he, 'hast thou forgot thy learning,   106
  Which hath it: The more perfect, the more keen,
  Whether for pleasure's or for pain's discerning?

Though true perfection never can be seen   109
  In these damned souls, they'll be more near complete
  After the Judgment than they yet have been.'

So, with more talk which I need not repeat,   112
  We followed the road that rings that circle round,
  Till on the next descent we set our feet;

There Pluto, the great enemy, we found.   115

THE IMAGES. *The Gluttonous*: The surrender to sin which
  began with mutual indulgence leads by an imperceptible

degradation to solitary self-indulgence. Of this kind of sin, the Gluttons are chosen as the image. Here is no reciprocity and no communication; each soul grovels alone in the mud, without heeding his neighbours – 'a sightless company', Dante calls them.

The Rain. Gluttony (like the other self-indulgences it typifies) often masquerades on earth as a warm, cosy, and indeed jolly kind of sin; here it is seen as it is – a cold sensuality, a sodden and filthy spiritual wretchedness.

Cerberus. In the *story*, Cerberus is the three-headed dog familiar to us from Homer and Virgil and the tale of the Twelve Labours of Hercules, who guards the threshold of the classical Hades. For the *allegory*, he is the image of uncontrolled appetite; the Glutton, whose appetite preyed upon people and things, is seen to be, in fact, the helpless prey on which that appetite gluts itself.

NOTES. l. 7: *I am now in the Third Circle*: Once again, Dante does not say how he got here: we may suppose that Virgil carried or assisted him down before he had wholly recovered his senses.

l. 22: *Worm*: This, in Old English as in Italian (*vermo*), is simply a word for a monster.

l. 26: *whole fistfuls of the miry ground*: To throw something into his mouth was the traditional way of appeasing this particular guardian of Hell – hence the phrase 'to give a sop to Cerberus'. In *Aeneid* VI, the Sibyl who guides Aeneas through Hades brings a number of cakes for the purpose. Here Virgil, not having made this provision, makes use of the first substitute that comes to hand.

l. 49: *thy native city*: Florence.

l. 52: *Ciacco you citizens nicknamed me*: The word means 'pig', and, according to Boccaccio, was the nickname of a Florentine gentleman notorious for his gluttony.

l. 61: *our distracted town*: i.e. Florence.

l. 64: *long time their strife will run its course*: This is the first of a number of passages dealing (under the guise of prophecy) with political events in Italy, and especially in Florence, which took place after the supposed date of the Vision (1300). It refers to the struggle between the two Guelf parties (the Blacks and the Whites), and to the final expulsion of the Whites (including Dante) from Florence.

l. 65: *the wood party*: the Whites. The adjective *selvaggia* means either the 'woodland' party (because certain of its leaders had come into Florence from the surrounding country) or the 'savage' (i.e. uncultivated) party (as opposed to the more aristocratic Blacks). The English word 'wood', which formerly had the meaning 'mad, wild, savage', is thus a fairly exact equivalent of the ambiguous Italian.

The two parties 'came to bloodshed' at the May-Day Festival of 1300, and the expulsion of the Black leaders took place shortly after. The Blacks returned in November 1301, with the help of Boniface VIII (the 'sitter on the fence', l. 69), who till then had shown no decided preference for either party. The first decree banishing the Whites was published in January 1302, and the last in the latter half of the same year – all 'within three suns' of the time at which Ciacco is supposed to be speaking.

l. 73: *two righteous men*: Dante is usually credited with meaning himself and his friend Guido Cavalcanti; but he

55

does not say so, and we need not found a charge of self-righteousness on what he has not said.

ll. 78–80: *Tegghiaio ... Mosca*: The persons named are all distinguished Florentines.

l. 96: *the Enemy Power*: This is the strangest and most terrible periphrasis used for Christ in these circles of the damned, who have chosen to know all goodness as antagonism and judgment.

l. 106: *thy learning*: the philosophy of Aristotle, as incorporated in the theology of St Thomas Aquinas. The souls will be 'more perfect' after the Last Judgment because they will then be reunited to their bodies.

l. 115: *Pluto*: God of the wealth that springs from the soil, he naturally came to be regarded as an 'underground' deity, and from early times was apt to be identified with Hades (Dis). Dante, however, distinguishes him from Dis (Satan), and while making him an infernal power, retains his primitive character as a symbol of riches. There is perhaps also a fusion with Plutus, the 'god of wealth' mentioned by Phaedrus. 'The great enemy' is probably an allusion to 1 *Tim.* VI. 10.

PENGUIN 60s CLASSICS

PENGUIN 60s CLASSICS

HENRY JAMES · *The Lesson of the Master*
FRANZ KAFKA · *The Judgement*
THOMAS À KEMPIS · *Counsels on the Spiritual Life*
HEINRICH VON KLEIST · *The Marquise of O—*
LIVY · *Hannibal's Crossing of the Alps*
NICCOLÒ MACHIAVELLI · *The Art of War*
SIR THOMAS MALORY · *The Death of King Arthur*
GUY DE MAUPASSANT · *Boule de Suif*
FRIEDRICH NIETZSCHE · *Zarathustra's Discourses*
OVID · *Orpheus in the Underworld*
PLATO · *Phaedrus*
EDGAR ALLAN POE · *The Murders in the Rue Morgue*
ARTHUR RIMBAUD · *A Season in Hell*
JEAN-JACQUES ROUSSEAU · *Meditations of a Solitary Walker*
ROBERT LOUIS STEVENSON · *Dr Jekyll and Mr Hyde*
TACITUS · *Nero and the Burning of Rome*
HENRY DAVID THOREAU · *Civil Disobedience*
LEO TOLSTOY · *The Death of Ivan Ilyich*
IVAN TURGENEV · *Three Sketches from a Hunter's Album*
MARK TWAIN · *The Man That Corrupted Hadleyburg*
GIORGIO VASARI · *Lives of Three Renaissance Artists*
EDITH WHARTON · *Souls Belated*
WALT WHITMAN · *Song of Myself*
OSCAR WILDE · *The Portrait of Mr W. H.*

ANONYMOUS WORKS

Beowulf and Grendel
Gilgamesh and Enkidu
Tales of Cú Chulaind

Buddha's Teachings
Krishna's Dialogue on the Soul
Two Viking Romances

READ MORE IN PENGUIN

For complete information about books available from Penguin and how to order them, please write to us at the appropriate address below. Please note that for copyright reasons the selection of books varies from country to country.

IN THE UNITED KINGDOM: Please write to *Dept. JC, Penguin Books Ltd, FREEPOST, West Drayton, Middlesex UB7 0BR.*
If you have any difficulty in obtaining a title, please send your order with the correct money, plus ten per cent for postage and packaging, to *PO Box No. 11, West Drayton, Middlesex UB7 0BR.*

IN THE UNITED STATES: Please write to *Consumer Sales, Penguin USA, P.O. Box 999, Dept. 17109, Bergenfield, New Jersey 07621-0120.* VISA and MasterCard holders call 1-800-253-6476 to order all Penguin titles.

IN CANADA: Please write to *Penguin Books Canada Ltd, 10 Alcorn Avenue, Suite 300, Toronto, Ontario M4V 3B2.*

IN AUSTRALIA: Please write to *Penguin Books Australia Ltd, P.O. Box 257, Ringwood, Victoria 3134.*

IN NEW ZEALAND: Please write to *Penguin Books (NZ) Ltd, Private Bag 102902, North Shore Mail Centre, Auckland 10.*

IN INDIA: Please write to *Penguin Books India Pvt Ltd, 706 Eros Apartments, 56 Nehru Place, New Delhi 110 019.*

IN THE NETHERLANDS: Please write to *Penguin Books Netherlands bv, Postbus 3507, NL-1001 AH Amsterdam.*

IN GERMANY: Please write to *Penguin Books Deutschland GmbH, Metzlerstrasse 26, 60594 Frankfurt am Main.*

IN SPAIN: Please write to *Penguin Books S. A., Bravo Murillo 19, 1° B, 28015 Madrid.*

IN ITALY: Please write to *Penguin Italia s.r.l., Via Felice Casati 20, I-20124 Milano.*

IN FRANCE: Please write to *Penguin France S. A., 17 rue Lejeune, F-31000 Toulouse.*

IN JAPAN: Please write to *Penguin Books Japan, Ishikiribashi Building, 2-5-4, Suido, Bunkyo-ku, Tokyo 112.*

IN GREECE: Please write to *Penguin Hellas Ltd, Dimocritou 3, GR-106 71 Athens.*

IN SOUTH AFRICA: Please write to *Longman Penguin Southern Africa (Pty) Ltd, Private Bag X08, Bertsham 2013.*